Karen

A very special gift for an extra
special person...
Wishing you a lifetime of happy
memories as you press upward & onward!

A favorite thought to share with you!

" WHAT LIES BEHIND US AND WHAT
LIES BEFORE US ARE SMALL
MATTERS COMPARED TO WHAT
LIES WITHIN US..."

RALPH WALDO EMERSON

love,
Tori

4/57

A GIFT OF PEACE

A GIFT OF PEACE

SELECTIONS FROM
A Course in Miracles

EDITED BY
Frances Vaughan, Ph.D.,
and
Roger Walsh, M.D., Ph.D.

PHOTOGRAPHS BY
Jane English, Ph.D.

JEREMY P. TARCHER, INC.
Los Angeles
Distributed by St. Martin's Press
New York

Dedicated to peace on earth.

Library of Congress Cataloging-in-Publication Data

A Gift of Peace.
Course in miracles. Selections.

1. Peace. I. Vaughan, Frances E. II. Walsh, Roger N.
BX9998.C6825 1986   230'.99   86-14343
ISBN 0-87477-398-9

Jeremy P. Tarcher, Inc.
9110 Sunset Blvd.
Los Angeles, CA 90069

Design by Tanya Maiboroda and Jane English

Manufactured in the United States of America
10 9 8 7 6 5 4 3 2 1

First Edition

CONTENTS

INTRODUCTION

Has there ever been a time in human history when the need for peace was greater? Each year new wars erupt, the arms race escalates, and a trillion dollars are spent on weapons, while millions of people remain hungry, helpless, and homeless.

Yet it is not that we are any more aggressive than our predecessors. Indeed, at this very moment millions of people are devoting their lives to calming hostilities, redressing injustices, and helping the poor and deprived. Rather, advances in technological power have awesomely magnified the impact of our negative states of mind. These negative states—such as emotions of greed and anger, thoughts of attack and revenge, and misperceptions of people and situations—are the root causes of the global problems we face today. The global turmoil mirrors our own inner turmoil, and the state of the world reflects the state of our minds.

Once this is recognized it becomes apparent that our global "problems" (nuclear weapons, ecological disturbances, mass starvation, etc.) are actually symptoms; symptoms of the psychological conflicts within us and between us. The basic source of our problems, as well as their solutions, lie within us, and therefore only solutions that include changing our minds are likely to be effective. Yet it is tragic how rarely this apparently obvious fact is recognized. Rather, most responses tend to be military, political, or economic and usually leave the psychological roots of the problems untouched or even exacerbated.

The question that therefore naturally arises (and it may be one of the most important questions of our time) is this: "What can we do to treat not only the global crises but also the deep psychological roots from which these crises arise?"

The great religions have addressed these root causes of suffering throughout human history. Each culture and age has brought forth its own version of the perennial wisdom that lies at the heart of the great religions. *A Course in Miracles* represents one form of this perennial wisdom for our own time. The significance and appeal of the *Course* transcend traditional boundaries and extend to all who ponder the deepest questions of human existence, meaning, and purpose. Its answers point out a path whereby the mind may be trained, our true identity remembered, and the gifts received thereby—such as love, joy, and peace—may be shared with the world.

The *Course* was first published in 1975 and consists of three volumes. The first is a text that lays out the underlying thought system; the second, a workbook with a lesson for each day of the year; and the third, a teacher's manual. The language of the *Course* is traditional in its use of Christian terminology and masculine pronouns, but the underlying message and principles are universal.

The central aim of the *Course* is peace. It offers a road map for finding the peace for which everyone yearns, which the world so desperately needs, and which religious sages throughout the ages have called "the highest form of happiness." "Forget not," it says, "that the motivation for this course is the attainment and the keeping of the state of peace."

The peace that the *Course* would have us experience is all encompassing, embracing our hearts and minds, our relationships, and the world. It points out that we cannot hope to create a peaceful world if we ourselves are not at peace. Peace, like love, it says, must first be uncovered within and then extended through our relationships in ever widening, ever more inclusive circles, until eventually peace encompasses everyone "without exception and without reserve." Moreover, this inner peace is not something that we must create but rather something that already exists within us as part of our true identity.

Recognizing this peace and extending it in the world requires removing the obstacles—the fears and fantasies, anger and aggression, defenses and distortions—that keep our true identity from being known to us. Moreover, as we relinquish these obstacles we discover that we never really needed them in the first place. Rather we find that our true Self has no need of anger, fear, or defensiveness and is naturally loving, joyous, and peaceful. Such is the central claim of *A Course in Miracles.*

To the extent that we recognize the love, joy, and peace that constitute our true identity, to that extent we desire to extend them through sharing them. Such sharing is both the means for, and the result of, removing the obstacles to the awareness of our Self and our inner peace. For *A Course in Miracles* suggests that what we give we receive, what we teach we learn, and as we see others we see ourselves. Therefore it recommends that we "learn that giving and receiving are the same," "teach peace to learn it," and "remember in your brother you but see yourself." Very simply, then, offering peace to others is a way to have it ourselves, and a natural result of having it is sharing it.

The following quotations from *A Course in Miracles* are those that we have found most relevant to the theme of peace. For those unfamiliar with the *Course,* we hope that *A Gift of Peace* may stimulate interest in exploring the original source. Certainly a full appreciation of the *Course* demands studying the original material since no quotations, no matter how beautiful, can offer more than a taste of the extraordinary depth and richness of the original. The potential impact of the *Course* can best be appreciated by studying it directly. If this book encourages readers to do that, it will have served its purpose well.

We are grateful for the opportunity of sharing these quotations and hope that they will indeed give you "a gift of peace" and enable you to share this gift with the world.

1

THE CHOICE
IS OURS

A Course in Miracles teaches that our choices and desires determine the nature and quality of our experience, behavior, relationships, and ultimately even our sense of identity. Moment by moment we choose whether to feel love or hate, whether to attack or forgive, whether to see truth or illusion. Each choice determines our perception of the meaning and purpose of our lives, and each choice is a decision for or against peace.

> *Peace will come to all who ask for it*
> *with real desire and sincerity of purpose.*

Deciding for Peace

This world will change through you.
No other means can save it.

Do you not think the world needs peace
as much as you do?
Do you not want to give it to the world
as much as you want to receive it?
For unless you do,
you will not receive it.

The question, "What do you want?"
must be answered.
You are answering it every minute
and every second,
and each moment of decision is a judgment
that is anything but ineffectual.
Its effects will follow automatically
until the decision is changed.

The power of decision is all that is yours.
What you can decide between is fixed,
because there are no alternatives
except truth and illusion.
And there is no overlap between them,
because they are opposites
which cannot be reconciled
and cannot both be true.
You are guilty or guiltless,
bound or free,
unhappy or happy.

What could you choose between
but life or death,
waking or sleeping,
peace or war,
your dreams or your reality?

Remember this: Every decision you make
stems from what you think you are,
and represents the value that
you put upon yourself.

Yet what you do not realize,
each time you choose,
is that your choice is your evaluation of yourself.

Every response you make
is determined by what you think you are,
and what you want to be
is what you think you are.
What you want to be, then,
must determine every response you make.

The power of your wanting
must first be recognized.
You must accept its strength, and not its weakness.
You must perceive that what is strong enough
to make a world can let it go,
and can accept correction
if it is willing to see that it was wrong.

Watch carefully and see what it is
you are really asking for.
Be very honest with yourself in this,
for we must hide nothing from each other.

Make, then, your choice.
But recognize that in this choice
the purpose of the world you see is chosen.

We choose again,
and make our choice for all our brothers,
knowing they are one with us.

This day I choose to spend in perfect peace.

The power of decision is my own.

Our Shared Purpose

"What for?"
This is the question that *you* must learn to ask
in connection with everything.
What is the purpose?
Whatever it is,
it will direct your efforts automatically.
When you make a decision of purpose,
then, you have made a decision
about your future effort;
a decision that will remain in effect
unless you change your mind.

Purpose is of the mind.
And minds can change as they desire.

Those who share a purpose have a mind as one.

The power of our joint motivation is beyond belief,
but not beyond accomplishment.
What we can accomplish together has no limits.

You will see your value
through your brother's eyes,
and each one is released as he beholds his savior
in place of the attacker whom he thought was there.
Through this releasing is the world released.
This is your part in bringing peace.
For you have asked what is your function here,
and have been answered.
Seek not to change it, nor to substitute another goal.
Accept this one and serve it willingly.

The goal is clear,
but now you need specific methods for attaining it.
The speed by which it can be reached
depends on this one thing alone;
your willingness to practice every step.
Each one will help a little,
every time it is attempted.
And together will these steps
lead you from dreams of judgment
to forgiving dreams and out of pain and fear.

We have a mission here.
We did not come to reinforce the madness
that we once believed in.
Let us not forget the goal that we accepted.
It is more than just our happiness alone
we came to gain.

Let me remember what my purpose is.

2

CHANGING YOUR MIND ABOUT YOUR MIND

Although the mind's natural state is one of peace, for most of us this peace lies hidden beneath the distorting veils of faulty perceptions, thoughts, and beliefs. Peace has become something that must be rediscovered and remembered through training the mind to correct its distortions. *A Course in Miracles* emphasizes that "an undisciplined mind can accomplish nothing" and that "this is a course in mind training." Only by training the mind to correct distorted thoughts and perceptions can the gift of peace be experienced.

Peace of mind is clearly an internal matter.
It must begin with your own thoughts,
and then extend outward.
It is from your peace of mind
that a peaceful perception of the world arises.

The Power of Mind

Your mind is the means
by which you determine your own condition,
because mind is the mechanism of decision.

You must learn to change your mind
about your mind.

Only your mind can produce fear.
It does so whenever it is conflicted in what it wants,
producing inevitable strain
because wanting and doing are discordant.

Only the mind can value,
and only the mind decides
on what it would receive and give.
And every gift it offers
depends on what it wants.

The world is nothing in itself.
Your mind must give it meaning.

You want to be happy.
You want peace.
You do not have them now,
because your mind is totally undisciplined.

Try to identify with the part of your mind
where stillness and peace reign forever.

Listen in deep silence.
Be very still and open your mind . . .
Sink deep into the peace that waits for you
beyond the frantic, riotous thoughts
and sights and sounds of this insane world.

There is a place in you
where there is perfect peace.
There is a place in you
where nothing is impossible.

The mind that serves spirit *is* invulnerable.

The mind which serves the spirit
is at peace and filled with joy.
Its power comes from spirit,
and it is fulfilling happily its function here.
Yet mind can also see itself divorced from spirit,
and perceive itself within a body
it confuses with itself.
Without its function then it has no peace,
and happiness is alien to its thoughts.

A tranquil mind is not a little gift.

Merely rest, alert but with no strain,
and let your mind in quietness be changed
so that the world is freed, along with you.

The mind which means that all it wants is peace
must join with other minds,
for that is how peace is obtained.
And when the wish for peace is genuine,
the means for finding it is given,
in a form each mind that seeks for it in honesty
can understand.

Alone we can do nothing,
but together our minds fuse into something
whose power is far beyond
the power of its separate parts.

Peace to my mind.
Let all my thoughts be still.

Perception Is a Mirror

You respond to what you perceive,
and as you perceive so shall you behave.

Every response you make
to everything you perceive
is up to you,
because your mind determines
your perception of it.

You cannot be aware without interpretation,
for what you perceive *is* your interpretation.

Understand that you do not respond
to anything directly,
but to your interpretation of it.
Your interpretation thus becomes
the justification for the response.

Perception selects, and makes the world you see.
It literally picks it out as the mind directs.
The laws of size and shape and brightness
would hold, perhaps,
if other things were equal.
They are not equal.
For what you look for
you are far more likely to discover
than what you would prefer to overlook.

The world can teach no images of you
unless you want to learn them.

Reality needs no cooperation from you to be itself.
But your awareness of it needs your help.

Perception is a choice
of what you want yourself to be;
the world you want to live in,
and the state in which you think your mind
will be content and satisfied.
It chooses where you think your safety lies,
at your decision.
It reveals yourself to you as you would have you be.
And always is it faithful to your purpose.

Let us be glad that you will see what you believe,
and that it has been given you to change
what you believe.

If you perceive truly
you are canceling out misperceptions
in yourself and in others simultaneously.
Because you see them as they are,
you offer them your acceptance of their truth
so they can accept it for themselves.

Let us not rest content
until the world has joined our changed perception.
Let us not be satisfied
until forgiveness has been made complete.

As I share the peace of the world with my brothers,
I begin to understand
that this peace comes from deep within myself.

The Power of Thought

Everything you see is the result of your thoughts.
There is no exception to this fact.

Every thought you have
brings either peace or war;
either love or fear.

From insane wishes comes an insane world.
From judgment comes a world condemned.
And from forgiving thoughts
a gentle world comes forth.

What you must recognize is
that when you do not share a thought system,
you are weakening it.
Those who believe in it
therefore perceive this as an attack on them.
This is because everyone identifies himself
with his thought system,
and every thought system centers
on what you believe you are.

You are free to believe what you choose,
and what you do attests to what you believe.

Let me look on the world I see
as the representation of my own state of mind.
I know that my state of mind can change,
and so I also know the world I see can change as well.

I have no neutral thoughts.

3

CHANGING WHAT YOU THINK IS REAL

The power of the mind is such that it can create whole worlds that appear to be real and outside us. This is most obvious in our sleeping dreams, which seem completely real to us when we are dreaming them. Only when we awaken do we recognize that all the people and things in the dream, including our own body, were actually created by our sleeping mind.

The *Course* suggests that the same is true of our usual waking state. It, too, is a dream from which we have not yet awakened. To awaken requires recognizing our dreams and illusions for what they really are and then being willing to relinquish them. In relinquishing our dreams we find reality and in reality we find peace.

Reality cannot "threaten" anything except illusions, since reality can only uphold truth.

Dreaming

Where are dreams but in a mind asleep?

You choose your dreams,
for they are what you wish,
perceived as if it had been given you.

You will first dream of peace,
and then awaken to it.
Your first exchange of what you made
for what you want
is the exchange of nightmares
for the happy dreams of love.

You recognize from your own experience
that what you see in dreams you think is real
while you are asleep.
Yet the instant you waken you realize
that everything that seemed to happen in the dream
did not happen at all.
You do not think this strange,
even though all the laws of what you awaken to
were violated while you slept.
Is it not possible that you merely shifted
from one dream to another,
without really waking?

Nothing in the world of dreams remains
without the hope of change and betterment,
for here is not where changelessness is found.
Let us be glad indeed that this is so,
and seek not the eternal in this world.
Forgiving dreams are means to step aside
from dreaming of a world outside yourself.
And leading finally beyond all dreams,
unto the peace of everlasting life.

Welcoming Reality

Real freedom depends on welcoming reality.

You do not have to seek reality.
It will seek you and find you
when you meet its conditions.

You cannot distort reality and know what it is.
And if you do distort reality you will experience
anxiety, depression and ultimately panic,
because you are trying to make yourself unreal.
When you feel these things,
do not try to look beyond yourself for truth,
for truth can only be within you.

It is not the reality of your brothers
or your Father or yourself that frightens you.
You do not know what they are,
and so you perceive them as ghosts
and monsters and dragons.

How does one overcome illusions?
Surely not by force or anger,
nor by opposing them in any way.
Merely by letting reason tell you
that they contradict reality.
They go against what must be true.
The opposition comes from them,
and not reality.
Reality opposes nothing.
What merely is needs no defense,
and offers none.
Only illusions need defense because of weakness.

Only reality is free of pain.
Only reality is free of loss.
Only reality is wholly safe.
And it is only this we seek today.

4

THE OBSTACLES
TO PEACE

We usually think of other people and outside events as the major obstacles to our peace. The *Course,* on the other hand, emphasizes that the major obstacles to peace reside within us as the emotions, thoughts, and beliefs that agitate our minds, cloud our perception, and distort our relationships. These barriers include emotions of fear and guilt, thoughts of judgment and condemnation, and mistaken beliefs in our specialness and in the value of sacrifice. We find peace when we release these emotions and question these beliefs, replacing fear and sacrifice with love and forgiveness.

Every obstacle that peace must flow across
is surmounted in just the same way;
the fear that raised it
yields to the love beyond,
and so the fear is gone.

The Pursuit of Specialness

The pursuit of specialness
is always at the cost of peace.

You are not special.
If you think you are,
and would defend your specialness
against the truth of what you really are,
how can you know the truth?

Specialness always makes comparisons.
It is established by a lack seen in another,
and maintained by searching for,
and keeping clear in sight,
all lacks it can perceive.

When peace is not with you entirely,
and when you suffer pain of any kind,
you have beheld some sin within your brother,
and have rejoiced at what you thought was there.
Your specialness seemed safe because of it.

The pursuit of specialness
must bring you pain.

Forgiveness is the end of specialness.
Only illusions can be forgiven,
and then they disappear.
Forgiveness is release from all illusion.

The Meaning of Sacrifice

The first illusion, which must be displaced
before another thought system can take hold,
is that it is a sacrifice
to give up the things of this world.
What could this be but an illusion,
since this world itself is nothing more than that?

Learn now that sacrifice of any kind
is nothing but a limitation imposed on giving.

Your confusion of sacrifice and love is so profound
that you cannot conceive of love without sacrifice.
And it is this that you must look upon;
sacrifice is attack, not love.
If you would accept but this one idea,
your fear of love would vanish.

You who believe that sacrifice is love
must learn that sacrifice is separation from love.
For sacrifice brings guilt
as surely as love brings peace.

It is not love that asks a sacrifice.
But fear demands the sacrifice of love,
for in love's presence fear cannot abide.

Let us join
in celebrating peace
by demanding
no sacrifice of anyone.

The Veil of Fear and Guilt

The first obstacle that peace must flow across
is your desire to get rid of it.
For it cannot extend unless you keep it.
You are the center from which it radiates outward,
to call the others in.
You are its home; its tranquil dwelling place
from which it gently reaches out,
but never leaving you.

If you are wholly free of fear of any kind,
and if all those who meet or even think of you
share your perfect peace,
then you can be sure
that you have learned God's lesson,
and not your own.

If you are fearful,
it is certain that you will endow the world
with attributes that it does not possess,
and crowd it with images that do not exist.

Truth is eclipsed by fear,
and what remains is but imagined.

Fear is a judgment never justified.
Its presence has no meaning but to show
you wrote a fearful script,
and are afraid accordingly.

Look at what you are afraid of.
Only the anticipation will frighten you.

How weak is fear;
how little and how meaningless.
How insignificant before the quiet strength
of those whom love has joined.

The journey that we undertake together
is the exchange of dark for light,
of ignorance for understanding.
Nothing you understand is fearful.

We go beyond the veil of fear,
lighting each other's way.

What is fear except love's absence?

Step back from fear,
and make advance to love.

Fear binds the world.
Forgiveness sets it free.

As love must look past fear,
so must fear see love not.
For love contains the end of guilt,
as surely as fear depends on it.

You think you hold against your brother
what he has done to you.
But what you really blame him for
is what *you* did to *him.*
It is not his past but yours
you hold against him.
And you lack faith in him
because of what you were.

Those whom you see as guilty
become the witnesses to guilt in you.

If you did not feel guilty
you could not attack,
for condemnation is the root of attack.
It is the judgment of one mind by another
as unworthy of love and deserving of punishment.

In any union with a brother
in which you seek to lay your guilt upon him,
or share it with him or perceive his own,
you will feel guilty.

Peace and guilt are antithetical.

The end of guilt will never come
as long as you believe there is a reason for it.
For you must learn
that guilt is always totally insane.

It is impossible to use one relationship
at the expense of another and not to suffer guilt.
And it is equally impossible
to condemn part of a relationship
and find peace within it.

Ask yourself honestly,
"Would I want to have perfect communication,
and am I wholly willing
to let everything that interferes with it go forever?"

Where there is communication
there is peace.

It is as sure that those who hold grievances
will suffer guilt,
as it is certain that those who forgive
will find peace.

Do not be afraid to look within.
The ego tells you
all is black with guilt within you,
and bids you not to look.
Instead, it bids you look upon your brothers,
and see the guilt in them.
Yet this you cannot do without remaining blind.

Only in your guiltlessness can you be happy.

Release from guilt as you would be released.

Fear is simply a mistake.
Let me not be afraid of truth today.

Releasing Judgment and Defense

The strain of constant judgment
is virtually intolerable.
It is curious that an ability so debilitating
would be so deeply cherished.

When you recognize what you are
and what your brothers are,
you will realize that judging them in any way
is without meaning. In fact,
their meaning is lost to you
precisely *because* you are judging them.

See yourself without condemnation,
by learning how to look on everything without it.

Instead of judging,
we need but be still
and let all things be healed.

Judgment and love are opposites.
From one come all the sorrows of the world.
But from the other comes the peace of God.

No one who loves can judge,
and what he sees is free of condemnation.

Judge not,
for you but judge yourself.

Those who believe that peace can be defended,
and that attack is justified on its behalf,
cannot perceive it lies within them.

Anger makes attack seem reasonable,
honestly provoked, and righteous
in the name of self-defense.
Yet is defensiveness a double threat.
For it attests to weakness,
and sets up a system of defense that cannot work.

A defense that cannot attack
is the best defense.

Truth has a power far beyond defense,
for no illusions can remain
where truth has been allowed to enter.
And it comes to any mind
that would lay down its arms,
and cease to play with folly.
It is found at any time;
today, if you will choose to practice
giving welcome to the truth.
This is our aim today.

Today we learn a lesson
which can save you more delay
and needless misery than you can possibly imagine.
It is this:
You make what you defend against, and by
Your own defense against it, is it real
And inescapable. Lay down your arms,
And only then do you perceive it false.

Help is here.
Learn to be quiet in the midst of turmoil,
for quietness is the end of strife
and this is the journey to peace.

How strong is he who comes without defenses,
offering only love's messages
to those who think he is their enemy.

If I defend myself I am attacked.
But in defenselessness I will be strong,
And I will learn what my defenses hide.

5

THE END OF
CONFLICT

Conflict and war in the world reflect conflict and war in the mind, and both this inner and this outer turmoil are born of thoughts of anger and attack. The relinquishment of anger and attack and the practice of forgiveness are, therefore, essential to the realization of peace both in the world and in ourselves.

Forgiveness ends the dream of conflict.

Reinterpreting Anger and Attack

Perhaps it will be helpful to remember
that no one can be angry at a fact.
It is always an interpretation
that gives rise to negative emotions,
regardless of their seeming justification
by what *appears* as facts.

If anger comes from an interpretation and not a fact,
it is never justified.
Once this is even dimly grasped,
the way is open.

When you are angry,
is it not because someone has failed
to fill the function you allotted him?
And does not this become the "reason"
your attack is justified?

Without projection there can be no anger,
but it is also true that without extension
there can be no love.

Accept only loving thoughts in others
and regard everything else as an appeal for help.

There is nothing to prevent you from recognizing
all calls for help as exactly what they are
except your own imagined need to attack.

If you attack error in another,
you will hurt yourself.
You cannot know your brother
when you attack him.
Attack is always made upon a stranger.
You are making him a stranger
by misperceiving him,
and so you cannot know him.
It is because you have made him a stranger
that you are afraid of him.
Perceive him correctly so that you can know him.

Because your attack thoughts will be projected,
you will fear attack.

Projection and attack are inevitably related,
because projection is always
a means of justifying attack.
Anger without projection is impossible.

Any concept of punishment
involves the projection of blame,
and reinforces the idea that blame is justified.
The result is a lesson in blame,
for all behavior teaches the beliefs that motivate it.

Those whom you perceive as opponents
are part of your peace,
which you are giving up by attacking them.

Safety is the complete relinquishment of attack.
No compromise is possible in this.
Teach attack in any form and you have learned it,
and it will hurt you.

The strong do not attack
because they see no need to do so.
Before the idea of attack can enter your mind,
you must have perceived yourself as weak.

Everyone here has entered darkness,
yet no one has entered it alone.
For he has come with Heaven's Help within him,
ready to lead him out of darkness
into light at any time.
The time he chooses can be any time,
for help is there, awaiting but his choice.
And when he chooses to avail himself
of what is given him,
then will he see each situation
that he thought before was means
to justify his anger
turned to an event which justifies his love.
He will hear plainly that the calls to war
he heard before are really calls to peace.
He will perceive that where he gave attack
is but another altar where he can,
with equal ease and far more happiness,
bestow forgiveness.
And he will reinterpret all temptation
as just another chance to bring him joy.

Joy goes with gentleness
as surely as grief attends attack.

The perfectly safe are wholly benign.
They bless because they know that they are blessed.

Today we . . . take a stand against our anger,
that our fears may disappear
and offer room to love.

Grievances are completely alien to love.
Grievances attack love and keep its light obscure.
If I hold grievances I am attacking love,
and therefore attacking my Self.

Without attack thoughts
I could not see a world of attack.
As forgiveness allows love
to return to my awareness,
I will see a world of peace and safety and joy.
And it is this I choose to see,
in place of what I look on now.

The Resolution of Conflict and War

Conflict is sleep, and peace awakening.

There must be doubt before there can be conflict.
And every doubt must be about yourself.

It is only the wish to deceive that makes war.
No one at one with himself
can even conceive of conflict.
Conflict is the inevitable result of self-deception,
and self-deception is dishonesty.

War is the condition in which fear is born,
and grows and seeks to dominate.
Peace is the state where love abides,
and seeks to share itself.
Conflict and peace are opposites.
Where one abides the other cannot be;
where either goes the other disappears.
So is the memory of God obscured in minds
that have become illusions' battleground.
Yet far beyond this senseless war it shines,
ready to be remembered when you side with peace.

Only the trusting can afford honesty,
for only they can see its value.
Honesty does not apply only to what you say.
The term actually means consistency.
There is nothing you say that contradicts
what you think or do;
no thought opposes any other thought;
no act belies your word;
and no word lacks agreement with another.
Such are the truly honest.
At no level are they in conflict with themselves.
Therefore it is impossible for them
to be in conflict with anyone or anything.

In quietness are all things answered,
and is every problem quietly resolved.
In conflict there can be no answer and no resolution,
for its purpose is to make no resolution possible,
and to ensure no answer will be plain.
A problem set in conflict has no answer,
for it is seen in different ways.
And what would be an answer
from one point of view
is not an answer in another light.

The conflict of illusions disappears
when it is brought to truth!
For it seems real only as long as it is seen
as war between conflicting truths . . .
Conflict is the choice between illusions,
one to be crowned as real,
the other vanquished and despised.

Illusions are but beliefs in what is not there.
And the seeming conflict between truth and illusion
can only be resolved by separating yourself
from the illusion and not the truth.

Illusion meets illusion; truth, itself.
The meeting of illusions leads to war.
Peace, looking on itself, extends itself.

I must have decided wrongly,
because I am not at peace.
I made the decision myself,
but I can also decide otherwise.
I want to decide otherwise,
because I want to be at peace.

6

PEACE TO MY BROTHER, WHO IS ONE WITH ME

A Course in Miracles suggests that we suffer from a case of mistaken identity. We have forgotten our true Self, which is said to be limitless, transcendent, and eternal. Instead we regard ourselves as an ego or separate self, limited to the body, fragile, ephemeral, and vulnerable. We therefore feel fearful and defensive, and regard the fleeting pleasures of the world as our only source of satisfaction.

Although all the great religious traditions help us recognize our true Self, the *Course* is unique in emphasizing relationships as the major means for this recognition. As we see and treat others, so do we see and treat ourselves. By recognizing the true Self in others we also find it in ourselves. A "holy relationship" is one that fosters this recognition and extends it in the world.

Remember in your brother you but see yourself.

The Errors of Ego

What is the ego?
But a dream of what you really are.

The ego is the mind's belief
that it is completely on its own.

Who asks you to define the ego
and explain how it arose
can be but he who thinks it real,
and seeks by definition to ensure
that its illusive nature is concealed
behind the words that seem to make it so.

Errors are of the ego,
and correction of errors
lies in the relinquishment of the ego.

Every response to the ego is a call to war,
and war does deprive you of peace.
Yet in this war there is no opponent.

Peace is the ego's greatest enemy because,
according to its interpretation of reality,
war is the guarantee of its survival.
The ego becomes strong in strife.

Even the wished-for can become unwelcome.
That must be so because the ego cannot be at peace.

When you are anxious,
realize that anxiety comes
from the capriciousness of the ego,
and *know this need not be.*
You can be as vigilant against the ego's dictates
as for them.

You Are One Self

You are one Self,
complete and healed and whole,
with power to lift the veil
of darkness from the world.

You are only love, but when you deny this,
you make what you are
something you must learn to remember.

You need to learn to lay all fear aside,
and know your Self as love
which has no opposite in you.

Fear not to look upon the lovely truth in you.

Your Self is still in peace,
even though your mind is in conflict.

Nothing outside yourself can save you;
nothing outside yourself can give you peace.

You will yet learn that peace is part of you,
and requires only that you be there
to embrace any situation in which you are.
And finally you will learn
that there is no limit to where you are,
so that your peace is everywhere,
as you are.

Limit the peace you share,
and your Self must be unknown to you.

What we accept as what we are proclaims
what everyone must be, along with us.
Fail not your brothers, or you fail yourself.
Look lovingly on them, that they may know
that they are part of you, and you of them.

*My Self is holy beyond all the thoughts of holiness
of which I now conceive.
Its shimmering and perfect purity
is far more brilliant
than is any light that I have ever looked upon.
Its love is limitless,
with an intensity that holds all things within it,
in the calm of quiet certainty.*

Knowing Your Brother

In learning to escape from illusions,
your debt to your brother is something
you must never forget.

Reason sees a holy relationship as what it is;
a common state of mind,
where both give errors gladly to correction,
that both may happily be healed as one.

Whenever you are with a brother,
you are learning what you are
because you are teaching what you are.
He will respond either with pain or with joy,
depending on which teacher you are following.
He will be imprisoned or released
according to your decision,
and so will you.
Never forget your responsibility to him,
because it is your responsibility to yourself.

Look gently on your brother,
and behold the world
in which perception of your hate
has been transformed into a world of love.

We begin the journey back by setting out together,
and gather in our brothers as we continue together.
Every gain in our strength is offered for all,
so they too can lay aside their weakness
and add their strength to us.

How can you find the way
except by taking your brother with you?

Everyone is looking for himself
and for the power and glory he thinks he has lost.
Whenever you are with anyone,
you have another opportunity to find them.

What you acknowledge in your brother
you are acknowledging in yourself,
and what you share you strengthen.

It will be given you to see your brother's worth
when all you want for him is peace.
And what you want for him
you will receive.

Look once again upon your brother,
not without the understanding
that he is the way to Heaven or to hell,
as you perceive him.
But forget not this;
the role you give to him is given you,
and you will walk the way you pointed out to him
because it is your judgment on yourself.

You who are the same
will not decide alone or differently.
Either you give each other life or death;
either you are each other's savior or his judge.

Through your gratitude
you come to know your brother,
and one moment of real recognition
makes everyone your brother.

Know your brother as yourself.
Answer his call for love,
and yours is answered.

To know your brother is to know God.

Each little gift you offer to your brother
lights up the world.

Nothing is asked of you
but to accept the changeless and eternal
that abide in him,
for your Identity is there.
The peace in you can but be found in him.
And every thought of love you offer him
but brings you nearer to your wakening
to peace eternal and to endless joy.

When you have seen your brothers as yourself
you will be released.

The quiet that surrounds you dwells in him,
and from this quiet come the happy dreams
in which your hands are joined in innocence.
These are not hands that grasp in dreams of pain.
They hold no sword,
for they have left their hold
on every vain illusion of this world.
And being empty they receive, instead,
a brother's hand in which completion lies.

This brother neither leads nor follows us,
but walks beside us on the selfsame road.
He is like us,
as near or far away from what we want
as we will let him be.
We make no gains he does not make with us,
and we fall back if he does not advance.
Take not his hand in anger but in love,
for in his progress do you count your own.

Have faith in him who walks with you,
so that your fearful concept of yourself may change.

Choose once again what you would have him be,
remembering that every choice you make
establishes your own identity
as you will see it and believe it is.

When you have become willing to hide nothing,
you will not only be willing
to enter into communion
but will also understand peace and joy.

From the oneness that we have attained
we call to all our brothers,
asking them to share our peace
and consummate our joy.

Let us celebrate our release together
by releasing everyone with us.

Let us unite in bringing blessing to the world.

Our function is to work together,
because apart from each other
we cannot function at all.
The whole power of God's Son
lies in all of us,
but not in any of us alone.

I would see you as my friend,
that I may remember you are part of me
and come to know myself.

Peace to my brother, who is one with me.
Let all the world be blessed with peace through us.

7

IT IS THROUGH US THAT PEACE WILL COME

The *Course* maintains that we are the essential instruments of peace for the world and that our own thoughts and actions determine how deeply peace is experienced and how widely it is shared. We become the means of peace when we are willing to learn, to teach, to give, and especially to forgive.

The *Course* is unique among spiritual paths in its emphasis on the importance of forgiveness for healing relationships. Forgiveness of both ourselves and others is said to be crucial for removing fear, anger, and all the other obstacles that distort our relationships and prevent us from experiencing peace in them.

> *This world will change through you.*
> *No other means can save it.*

To Teach Is to Learn

The only way to have peace is to teach peace.
By teaching peace you must learn it yourself.

In the teaching-learning situation, each one
learns that giving and receiving are the same.
The demarcations they have drawn
between their roles, their minds, their bodies,
their needs, their interests, and all the differences
they thought separated them from one another,
fade and grow dim and disappear.

All good teachers realize
that only fundamental change will last,
but they do not begin at that level.
Strengthening motivation for change
is their first and foremost goal.
It is also their last and final one.
Increasing motivation for change in the learner
is all that a teacher need do to guarantee change.
Change in motivation is a change of mind,
and this will inevitably produce fundamental change
because the mind *is* fundamental.

Your past learning
must have taught you the wrong things,
simply because it has not made you happy.
On this basis alone its value should be questioned.

Understand you but waste time
unless you go beyond what you have learned
to what is yet to learn.

A wise teacher teaches through approach,
not avoidance.
He does not emphasize what you must avoid
to escape from harm,
but what you need to learn to have joy.

Correct and learn, and be open to learning.
You have not made truth,
but truth can still set you free.

To Give Is to Receive

Offer peace to have it yours.

Each gift is an evaluation
of the receiver and the *giver*.

You can give yourself completely,
wholly without loss and only with gain.
Herein lies peace,
for here there *is* no conflict.

Those who offer peace to everyone
have found a home in Heaven
the world cannot destroy.
For it is large enough
to hold the world within its peace.

*Today we will attempt to offer peace to everyone,
and see how quickly peace returns to us.*

I am here only to be truly helpful.

To Let Forgiveness Rest upon All Things

Where could your peace arise
but from forgiveness?

Forgiveness removes only the untrue,
lifting the shadows from the world and carrying it,
safe and sure within its gentleness,
to the bright world of new and clean perception.
There is your purpose *now.*
And it is there that peace awaits you.

Look upon the world with forgiving eyes.
For forgiveness literally transforms vision,
and lets you see the real world
reaching quietly and gently across chaos,
removing all illusions
that had twisted your perception
and fixed it on the past.

To forgive is merely to remember
only the loving thoughts you gave in the past,
and those that were given you.
All the rest must be forgotten.

All that must be forgiven are the illusions
you have held against your brother.

Withhold forgiveness from your brother
and you attack him.
You give him nothing,
and receive of him but what you gave.

Those you do not forgive you fear.

Forgiveness cannot be withheld a little.
Nor is it possible to attack for this and love for that
and understand forgiveness.

Whom you forgive is free,
and what you give you share.
Forgive the sins your brother
thinks he has committed,
and all the guilt you think you see in him.

Forgiveness takes away
what stands between your brother and yourself.
It is the wish that you be joined with him,
and not apart.

Who forgives is healed.
And in his healing lies the proof
that he has truly pardoned,
and retains no trace of condemnation
that he still would hold
against himself or any living thing.

Make way for love, which you did not create,
but which you can extend.
On earth this means forgive your brother,
that the darkness may be lifted from your mind.

How willing are you to forgive your brother?
How much do you desire peace
instead of endless strife and misery and pain?
These questions are the same,
in different form.
Forgiveness is your peace,
for herein lies the end of separation
and the dream of danger and destruction.

If you can see your brother merits pardon,
you have learned forgiveness is your right
as much as his.

You are merely asked to see forgiveness
as the natural reaction
to distress that rests on error,
and thus calls for help.
Forgiveness is the only sane response.

Without forgiveness is the mind in chains,
believing in its own futility.
Yet with forgiveness does the light
shine through the dream of darkness.

The unforgiving mind is full of fear,
and offers love no room to be itself;
no place where it can spread its wings in peace
and soar above the turmoil of the world.
The unforgiving mind is sad,
without the hope of respite and release from pain.
It suffers and abides in misery,
peering about in darkness, seeing not,
yet certain of the danger lurking there.

An unforgiving thought
is one which makes a judgment
that it will not raise to doubt,
although it is not true.
The mind is closed, and will not be released.
The thought protects projection,
tightening its chains,
so that distortions are more veiled
and more obscure; less easily accessible to doubt,
and further kept from reason.

An unforgiving thought does many things.
In frantic action it pursues its goal,
twisting and overturning what it sees
as interfering with its chosen path.
Distortion is its purpose, and the means
by which it would accomplish it as well.
It sets about its furious attempts to smash reality,
without concern for anything that would appear
to pose a contradiction to its point of view.
Forgiveness, on the other hand,
is still, and quietly does nothing.
It offends no aspect of reality,
nor seeks to twist it to appearances it likes.
It merely looks, and waits, and judges not.

There can be no form of suffering
that fails to hide an unforgiving thought.
Nor can there be a form of pain
forgiveness cannot heal.

Forgiveness paints a picture of a world
where suffering is over, loss becomes impossible
and anger makes no sense.
Attack is gone, and madness has an end.

Fear condemns and love forgives.
Forgiveness thus undoes
what fear has produced.

Today we practice true forgiveness,
that the time of joining be no more delayed.

When I have forgiven myself
and remembered who I am,
I will bless everyone and everything I see.

To Bring Peace to the World

This world has much to offer to your peace,
and many chances to extend your own forgiveness.
Such its purpose is,
to those who want to see
peace and forgiveness descend on them,
and offer them the light.

You are entrusted with
the world's release from pain.

The part you play
in salvaging the world from condemnation
is your own escape.

This world awaits the freedom you will give
when you have recognized that you are free.

What cause have you for anger in a world
that merely waits your blessing to be free?

Until forgiveness is complete,
the world does have a purpose.
It becomes the home in which forgiveness is born,
and where it grows and becomes stronger
and more all-embracing.
Here is it nourished, for here it is needed.

We will forgive them all,
absolving all the world
from what we thought it did to us.
For it is we who make the world
as we would have it.

A world in which forgiveness shines on everything,
and peace offers its gentle light to everyone,
is inconceivable to those
who see a world of hatred rising from attack,
poised to avenge, to murder and destroy.
Yet is the world of hatred equally unseen
and inconceivable to those
who feel God's love in them.
Their world reflects the quietness and peace
that shines in them;
the gentleness and innocence
they see surrounding them;
the joy with which they look out
from the endless wells of joy within.
What they have felt in them they look upon,
and see its sure reflection everywhere.

What would you see?
The choice is given you.
But learn and do not let your mind forget
this law of seeing:
You will look upon that which you feel within.
If hatred finds a place within your heart,
you will perceive a fearful world,
held cruelly in death's sharp-pointed, bony fingers.
If you feel the Love of God within you,
you will look out on a world of mercy and of love.

If you choose to see a world without an enemy,
in which you are not helpless,
the means to see it will be given you.

No longer is the world our enemy,
for we have chosen that we be its Friend.

My forgiveness is the means
by which the world is healed,
together with myself.
Let me then, forgive the world,
that it may be healed along with me.

8

THE GIFTS OF PEACE

When peace is welcomed, it brings with it many gifts, among them healing, freedom, and love. Like peace, these gifts cannot be kept for ourselves alone but rather must be shared with others if we are to know them as our own.

You understand that you are healed
when you give healing.
You accept forgiveness as accomplished in yourself
when you forgive.
You recognize your brother as yourself,
and thus do you perceive that you are whole.

Healing

Peace must come to those who choose to heal
and not to judge.

The decision to heal and to be healed
is the first step toward recognizing
what you truly want.
Every attack is a step away from this,
and every healing thought brings it closer.

Healing will flash across your open mind,
as peace and truth arise
to take the place of war and vain imaginings.

Healing is release from the fear of waking
and the substitution of the decision to wake.
The decision to wake
is the reflection of the will to love,
since all healing involves replacing fear with love.

Would you not prefer to heal
what has been broken,
and join in making whole
what has been ravaged by separation and disease?
You have been called,
together with your brother,
to the most holy function this world contains.
It is the only one that has no limits,
and reaches out to every broken
fragment of the Sonship
with healing and uniting comfort.

You will be made whole
As you make whole.

No one can ask another to be healed.
But he can let *himself* be healed,
and thus offer the other what he has received.
Who can bestow upon another
what he does not have?
And who can share what he denies himself?

Those whom you heal bear witness to your healing,
for in their wholeness you will see your own.

We will try today to find the source of healing,
which is in our minds. . . .
It is not farther from us than ourselves.
It is as near to us as our own thoughts;
so close it is impossible to lose.
We need but seek it, and it must be found.

Our function is to let our minds be healed,
that we may carry healing to the world,
exchanging curse for blessing, pain for joy,
and separation for the peace of God.

Peace fills my heart,
and floods my body
with the purpose of forgiveness.
Now my mind is healed.

Freedom

Who could be set free
while he imprisons anyone?
A jailer is not free,
for he is bound together with his prisoner.

Look about the world,
and see the suffering there.
Is not your heart willing
to bring your weary brothers rest?
They must await your own release.
They stay in chains till you are free.
They cannot see the mercy of the world
until you find it in yourself.

In your freedom lies the freedom of the world.

You can escape all bondage of the world,
and give the world the same release you found.
You can remember what the world forgot,
and offer it your own remembering.

As we offer freedom,
it is given us.

Love

In honesty, is it not harder for you to say
"I love" than "I hate"?
You associate love with weakness
and hatred with strength,
and your own real power seems to you
as your real weakness.
For you could not control
your joyous response to the call of love
if you heard it.

By not offering total love
you will not be healed completely.

Love always answers,
being unable to deny a call for help,
or not to hear the cries of pain that rise to it
from every part of this strange world.

The opposite of love is fear,
but what is all encompassing
can have no opposite.

Perfect love casts out fear.
If fear exists,
Then there is not perfect love.

Whenever you are not wholly joyous,
it is because you have reacted with a lack of love.

You have so little faith in yourself
because you are unwilling to accept the fact
that perfect love is in you.
And so you seek without
for what you cannot find without.

Everyone seeks for love as you do,
but knows it not unless he joins with you
in seeking it.

The attraction of love for love
remains irresistible.
For it is the function of love
to unite all things unto itself,
and to hold all things together
by extending its wholeness.

As you release, so will you be released.
Forget this not,
or love will be unable
to find you and comfort you.

Love's arms are open to receive you,
and give you peace forever.

Love wishes to be known,
completely understood and shared.
It has no secrets;
nothing that it would keep apart and hide.

Love does not seek for power,
but for relationships.

Truth does not struggle against ignorance,
and love does not attack fear.

Love can have no enemy.

Be not afraid of love.
For it alone can heal all sorrow.

Fail not in your function
of loving in a loveless place
made out of darkness and deceit,
for thus are darkness and deceit undone.

The holiest of all the spots on earth
is where an ancient hatred
has become a present love.

Love cannot be far behind
a grateful heart and thankful mind.

There is no room in us for fear today,
for we have welcomed love into our hearts.

We are deceived no longer.
Love has now returned to our awareness.
And we are at peace again,
for fear has gone and only love remains.

Love holds no grievances.
When I let all my grievances go
I will know I am perfectly safe.

The Way to Peace
Is Open

The way to peace is open, but each of us must choose whether or not to follow it. The *Course* suggests, however, that our final choice is certain, since peace is truly our deepest desire and the only alternative is to languish in dreams of pain and conflict. We can delay, but why would we want to, when on our choice rests the welfare and peace of the world and when peace is freely available for all.

> *Make way for peace*
> *and it will come.*

The Way to Peace Is Open

There is a silence
into which the world cannot intrude.
There is an ancient peace
you carry in your heart
and have not lost.

Peace is a natural heritage of spirit.
Everyone is free to refuse to accept his inheritance,
but he is not free to establish
what his inheritance is.

Peace and understanding go together
and never can be found alone.

Strength and innocence are not in conflict,
but naturally live in peace.

Lay down your arms,
and come without defense into the quiet place
where Heaven's peace holds all things still at last.
Lay down all thoughts of danger and of fear.
Let no attack enter with you.

In this quiet state alone
is strength and power.
Here can no weakness enter,
for here is no attack
and therefore no illusions.

Peace is, of God.
You who are part of God
are not at home except in His peace.

Abide in peace,
where God would have you be.

God knows you only in peace,
and this is your reality.

His peace surrounds you silently.
God is very quiet.

Look with peace upon your brothers,
and God will come rushing into your heart
in gratitude for your gift to Him.

The peace of God passeth your understanding
only in the past.
Yet here it *is,*
and you can understand it *now.*

"I want the peace of God."
To say these words is nothing.
But to mean these words is everything. . . .
No one can mean these words and not be healed.
He cannot play with dreams,
nor think he is himself a dream.
He cannot make a hell and think it real.
He wants the peace of God,
and it is given him.
For that is all he wants,
and that is all he will receive.
Many have said these words.
But few indeed have meant them.
You have but to look upon
the world you see around you
to be sure how very few they are.

We want the peace of God.
This is no idle wish.
These words do not request
another dream be given us.
They do not ask for compromise,
nor try to make another bargain in the hope
that there may yet be one that can succeed
where all the rest have failed.
To mean these words acknowledges
illusions are in vain,
requesting the eternal in the place of shifting dreams
which seem to change in what they offer,
but are one in nothingness.

"There is no peace except the peace of God."
Seek you no further.
You will not find peace
except the peace of God.
Accept this fact,
and save yourself the agony
of yet more bitter disappointments, bleak despair,
and sense of icy hopelessness and doubt.
Seek you no further.
There is nothing else for you to find
except the peace of God.

REFERENCES

To facilitate further study, we have referenced each passage included in this book, citing the volume and page number from which it was excerpted. WB stands for Workbook, T for Text, and MT for Manual for Teachers. A Course in Miracles *(three hard-cover books) may be ordered from Foundation for Peace, P.O. Box 635, Tiburon, California 94920. Price is $40. All three books are also available in a single soft-cover volume for $25. California residents add 6% sales tax. A cassette tape of readings from* A Gift of Peace *by Frances Vaughan is available for $9 plus tax from Miracle Distribution Center, 1141 East Ash Avenue, Fullerton, California 92631.*

THE CHOICE IS OURS

T 412. *Deciding for Peace:* WB 220; T 134; T 78; T 255; T 541; T 285; T 285; T 118; T 418; T 56; T 489; WB 320; T 489; WB 274. *Our Shared Purpose:* T 61; T 472; T 463; T 71; T 448–449; T 581; WB 261; WB 413.

CHANGING YOUR MIND ABOUT YOUR MIND

WB 51. *The Power of Mind:* T 134; T 113; T 26; T 397; WB 236; WB 31; WB 78; WB 78; WB 76; T 9; WB 167; MT 49; WB 238; WB 339–340; T 136; WB 392. *Perception Is a Mirror:* T 7; T 168; T 192; T 200; T 425; T 613; T 425; T 483; T 607; T 35; WB 403; WB 94. *The Power of Thought:* WB 26; WB 26; WB 454; T 98; T 5; WB 87; WB 26.

CHANGING WHAT YOU THINK IS REAL

T 149. *Dreaming:* T 574; T 574; T 238; T 169; T 571–572; WB 427; T 569; T 568; WB 193. *The Cost of Illusions:* T 320; T 118; T 231; T 229; T 461; T 315; T 385; T 315; WB 128; T 325; T 446–447; T 562; MT 87; WB 189. *Letting Go of the Past:* T 240; T 574; T 234; T 234; T 324; T 324; WB 130; T 325; T 292; T 282; T 281; T 234–235; T 281–282; WB 195; T 604; T 280; T 386; MT 58. *Welcoming Reality:* T 184; T 146; T 152; T 198; T 445; WB 419.

THE OBSTACLES TO PEACE

T 392. *The Pursuit of Specialness:* T 467; T 467; T 466; T 473; T 467; T 470. *The Meaning of Sacrifice:* MT 32; T 302; T 302; T 304–305; T 564; T 306. *The Veil of Fear and Guilt:* T 380; T 276; WB 21; WB 231; T 596; T 240; T 446; T 264; T 399; WB 403; WB 365; WB 458; T 382; T 344; T 244; T 220; T 245; T 221; T 246; T 292; T 289; T 305; WB 114; T 244; T 255; T 247; WB 428. *Releasing Judgment and Defense:* T 43; T 42; T 156; WB 389; WB 470; T 411; MT 37; T 461; WB 277; T 17; WB 252; WB 318; T 204; WB 332; WB 248.

THE END OF CONFLICT

WB 459. *Reinterpreting Anger and Attack:* MT 42; MT 44; T 569; T 120; T 202; T 200; T 37; WB 40; T 89; T 88; T 128; T 92; T 209; T 488; MT 12; T 92; WB 297; WB 147; WB 89. *The Resolution of Conflict and War:* WB 458; T 475; MT 11; T 455; MT 10; T 533; T 454; T 312; T 454; T 83.

PEACE TO MY BROTHER, WHO IS ONE WITH ME

WB 292. *The Errors of Ego:* MT 77; T 53; MT 77; T 155; T 128; T 73; MT 79; T 57. *You Are One Self:* WB 166; T 92; T 246; WB 175; T 46; WB 118; WB 80; T 186; WB 261; WB 410. *Knowing Your Brother:* T 61; T 444; T 132; T 513; T 137; T 76; T 132; T 72; T 405; T 492; T 440; T 63; T 203; T 62; T 449; T 570; T 242; T 571; T 604; T 616; T 621; T 8; WB 469; T 304; T 518; T 139; WB 115; WB 474.

IT IS THROUGH US THAT PEACE WILL COME

WB 220. *To Teach Is to Learn:* T 92; MT 5; T 98–99; T 128; T 608; T 96; T 74. *To Give Is to Receive:* T 617; T 397; T 293; T 490; WB 192; T 24. *To Let Forgiveness Rest upon All Things:* T 473; T 370; T 329; T 330; T 325; T 460; T 393; T 461; T 394; T 516; T 528; T 568; T 572; T 594; T 593; WB 458; WB 210; WB 391; WB 391; WB 370; WB 408; WB 73; WB 244; WB 83. *To Bring Peace to the World:* T 488; WB 310; T 540; T 585; T 585; MT 35; WB 348; WB 349; WB 349; T 432; WB 361; WB 145.

THE GIFTS OF PEACE

WB 293. *Healing:* T 434; T 182; WB 252; T 147; T 350; T 203; T 535; T 235; WB 264; WB 255–256; WB 419. *Freedom:* WB 356; WB 354; WB 48; WB 335; WB 458. *Love:* T 226; T 227; T 237; T Intro; T 12; T 82; T 293; T 274; T 219; T 321; T 408; T 407; T 407; T 267; WB 231; WB 445; T 260; T 522; MT 55; WB 444; WB 453; WB 115.

THE WAY TO PEACE IS OPEN

T 279. *The Way to Peace Is Open:* WB 304; T 44; T 278; T 33; WB 352; T 446; T 74; T 518; T 39; T 184; T 177; T 238; WB 339; WB 340; WB 374.

OTHER BOOKS BY THE EDITORS AND PHOTOGRAPHER

Accept This Gift: Selections from A Course in Miracles
Beyond Ego: Transpersonal Dimensions in Psychology

By Frances Vaughan

Awakening Intuition

*The Inward Arc: Healing and Wholeness in Psychotherapy
and Spirituality*

By Roger Walsh

*Beyond Health and Normality: Explorations of Exceptional
Psychological Well-Being* (with D.H. Shapiro)

Meditation: Classic and Contemporary Perspectives
(with D.H. Shapiro)

Staying Alive: The Psychology of Human Survival

Illustrated by Jane English

Tao Te Ching-Lao Tsu (with Gia-Fu Feng)
Chuang Tsu-Inner Chapters (with Gia-Fu Feng)
Waterchild (with Judith Bolinger)

Written by Jane English

Different Doorway: Adventures of a Caesarean Born